ROSE IS ROSE

15TH ANNIVERSARY COLLECTION

BY

PAT BRADY

Andrews McMeel
Publishing

Kansas City

www.andrewsmcmeel.com

99 00 01 02 03 BAH 10 9 8 7 6 5 4 3 2 1

ISBN: 0-8362-8196-9

Library of Congress Catalog Card Number: 98-88671

Enjoy More **Rose is Rose** Collections from Andrews McMeel Publishing

For ordering information, call 1-800-826-4216

E-mail Pat Brady at: PBradyRose@aol.com

Read *Rose is Rose* on the World Wide Web at: http://www.comics.com

Shop for *Rose is Rose* merchandise online at http://www.umstore.com

4

HUG BANDITS

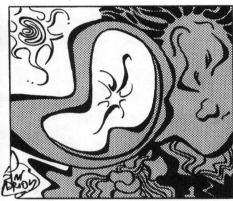

THE CRAYON'S EYE VIEW
OF THE MAGNIFYING GLASS —
SOLAR HEAT EXPERIMENT

TROLLING FOR SCRITCHES

SCRITCH
SCRITCH
SCRITCH
SCRITCH
SCRITCH

I CAME INTO THIS ROOM FOR A REASON, AND NOW I CAN'T REMEMBER WHAT IT WAS!

ME TOO!

THE OLDER I GET, THE MORE FREQUENTLY THIS HAPPENS!

SAME HERE!

I HEAR THERE'S A LOT OF ROMANCE AMONG SENIOR CITIZENS!

THE OPPORTUNITIES ARE CERTAINLY THERE!

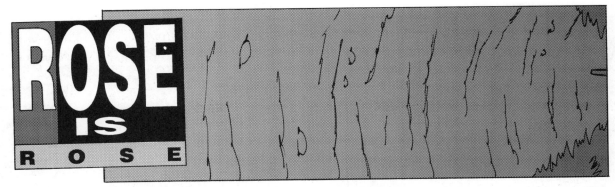

ROSE IS ROSE

YOU'RE ANGRY AT CLEM FOR GOOD REASON, PASQUALE...

BUT TRY TO FORGIVE, OR ELSE YOU'LL DESCEND INTO THE DUNGEON OF RESENTMENT...

I KNOW, BECAUSE I'VE BEEN THERE MYSELF MANY TIMES!

BOING

I GO THERE TOO, I JUST DON'T STAY AS LONG AS YOU DO!

ROSE IS
ROSE

19

YOGA MASTER MAHARISHI PEEKABOO STRETCHES HER DISCIPLINED BODY ...

:YAWN:

SHE OPENS HER SEVEN ENERGY CENTERS WITH DEEP BREATHING ...

PURRR PURRR PURRR

AND... CHANTING HER ANCIENT HYMN ...

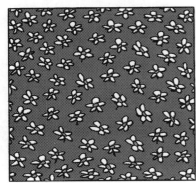

SHE BECOMES ONE WITH THE UNIVERSE.

WHERE'S PEEKABOO?

OH, HEAVEN KNOWS! SHE'S A MASTER AT DISAPPEARING!

21

PEEKABOO IS TEARING AROUND THE HOUSE FOR NO KNOWN REASON AGAIN!

I HOPE SHE DOESN'T WAKE PASQUALE!

A "DREAMSHIP'S "ENLARGE" BUTTON PROVIDES SAFETY, BUT SACRIFICES MANEUVERABILITY.

PEEKABOO, GET OFF ME! YOU KEPT ME AWAKE ALL NIGHT!

GOOD MORNING! BE NICE, PASQUALE...

WAKE HER GENTLY... SHE PROBABLY HAS BEEN HAVING A COOL DREAM!

BLINK BLINK

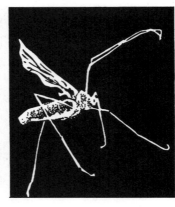

24

ROSE IS ROSE

26

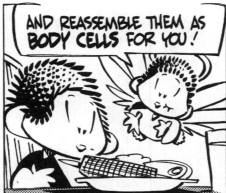

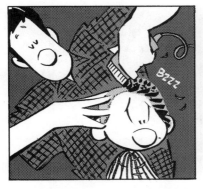

ROSE IS ROSE

IT IS POSSIBLE TO
STAY OUT OF RANGE
OF GARLIC BREATH.

GARLIC **BURPS**
ARE ANOTHER MATTER.

SNIFF
SNIFF

IT SMELLS LIKE PASQUALE
IS UNDER THE BED!

LET
HIM
STAY
THERE!

IN HIDE-AND-SEEK,
GARLIC BREATH IS
A MIXED BLESSING

GRASSHOPPER'S VIEW OF
A PICNIC FROM THE
RIM OF A SODA CAN

YOGA MASTER MAHARISHI PEEKABOO PERFORMS A DEMONSTRATION FOR A DEVOTEE.

AFTERWARDS, THE MASTER SEEKS SOLITUDE.

HEY! WHERE ARE YOU GOING?

CLINGY DEVOTEES ARE A FACT OF LIFE FOR MAHARISHIS.

AFTER MANY GRUELING HOURS OF SOLITARY MEDITATION...

YOGA MASTER MAHARISHI PEEKABOO EXPERIENCES A **BRILLIANT FLASH OF** –

THERE YOU ARE!

A REALLY CLINGY DEVOTEE CAN GET ON A MAHARISHI'S NERVES.

I'VE NEVER BEEN SO CONTENT AS I AM AT THIS MOMENT!

BUT I WONDER HOW LONG IT CAN **LAST**?!

IS THERE A SECRET TO MAKING IT LAST FOREVER? DO YOU KNOW THE SECRET?

YES...

...DON'T **WORRY** ABOUT IT!

TOO LATE!

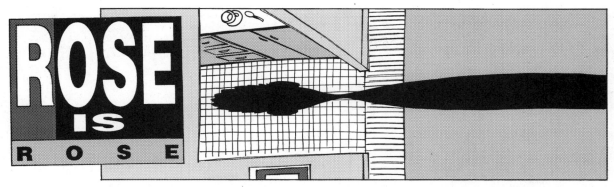

ROSE HAS ACCIDENTALLY EATEN A JALAPEÑO PEPPER, CAUSING THE EMERGENCE OF HER ALTER EGO, VICKI THE BIKER...

REACTING TO THE TASTE OF A JALAPEÑO PEPPER, ROSE HEADS INTO TOWN AS HER ALTER EGO, VICKI THE BIKER!

WHAT'LL IT BE?

FROOT LOOPS?

EVENTUALLY THE TASTE OF A JALAPEÑO PEPPER FADES AWAY.

YOU DON'T LOOK LIKE ONE OF THE REGULARS HERE!

I'M NOT! ALL I REMEMBER IS, I ATE A JALAPEÑO PEPPER AND...

:BURP:

AND?

AND HERE WE GO AGAIN!

THIS IS YOUR "MOTOR-CYCLE"?

IT WAS, AFTER I ATE A JALAPEÑO!

TAKE CARE! COME BACK AND SEE US AFTER YOUR NEXT JALAPEÑO!

LATER...

MMM... CHOCOLATE MILK!

MAYBE IF I PUT A JALAPEÑO IN CHOCOLATE MILK, THE EFFECTS WOULD CANCEL EACH OTHER OUT!

HIDE AND SEEK: CLEM'S PERSONAL BEST

BOOM

FLUTTER

WHEN YOU FLUTTERED YOUR EYELASHES, LIGHTNING FLASHED AND THUNDER ROLLED!

UNLESS I IMAGINED IT!

EITHER WAY SOUNDS GREAT TO ME!

AMAZING! WHEN YOU FLUTTERED YOUR EYELASHES, THUNDER AND LIGHTNING HAPPENED!

WHAT A ROMANTIC COINCIDENCE!

BOOM

DID YOU JUST FLUTTER AGAIN?

I'D BE A FOOL TO DENY IT!

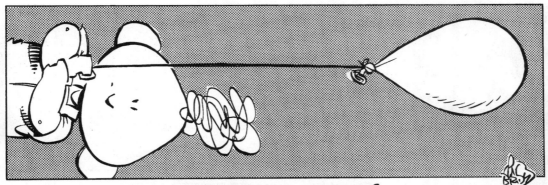

CLEM HOLDING A HELIUM BALLOON, WAITING FOR PASQUALE TO COME OUT AND PLAY

CLEM HANGING FROM A TREE LIMB BY HIS KNEES WITH A WATER BALLOON, WAITING FOR PASQUALE TO COME OUT AND PLAY

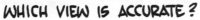

WHICH VIEW IS ACCURATE?

CLOTHESPINS AND STRING SHOULD WORK!

REMEMBER, AFTER JUMP-STARTING A SMILE, YOU SHOULD LET IT RUN FOR TWENTY MINUTES.

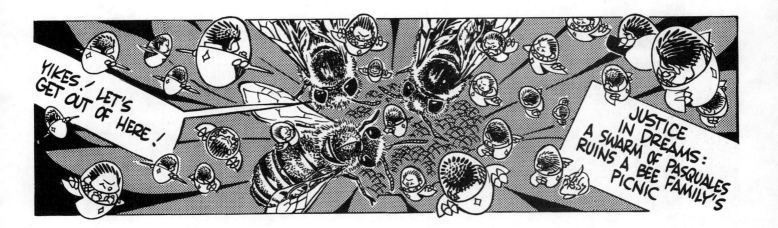

YIKES! LET'S GET OUT OF HERE!

JUSTICE IN DREAMS: A SWARM OF PASQUALES RUINS A BEE FAMILY'S PICNIC

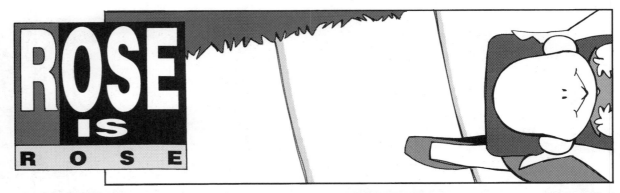

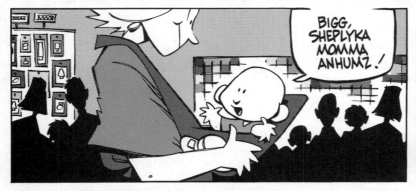

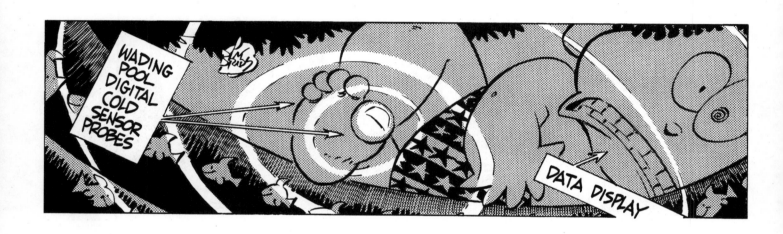

OSCILLATING FAN'S EYE VIEW

OSCILLATING FAN, TOP VIEW

OOF! THIS MIRROR IS HEAVY!

MAYBE WE SHOULD GET OUT OF IT BEFORE WE LIFT IT!

OOF! IT'S NO LIGHTER FROM THIS SIDE!

WELL, NOW THE WHOLE BEDROOM IS IN IT!

43

:WAD:
:SQUEEZE:

:SQUEEZE:
:WAD:

DO YOU REALIZE HOW MUCH WASTED SPACE THERE IS IN A LOAF OF BREAD?

SEE, I SQUEEZED AN ENTIRE LOAF OF BREAD INTO ONE CONVENIENT WAD!

THINK OF ALL THE KITCHEN SPACE I SAVED YOU!

YES, AND I JUST THOUGHT OF A WAY TO SAVE EVEN MORE!

HOW?

CLOSE ENCOUNTERS OF THE FREEWAY KIND

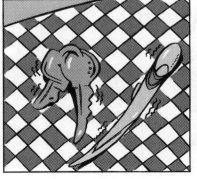

PEEKABOO, ABDUCTED BY ANOTHER LIFE FORM, FINDS HERSELF IN A SMALL, WOBBLY TRANSPORT POD...

TENSE FACES OF OTHER ABDUCTEES EMERGE FROM INSIDE SIMILAR PODS...

REPRESSED MEMORIES OF PAST ABDUCTIONS BEGIN TO SURFACE...

THE HATCH OF THE TRANSPORT POD OPENS TO REVEAL A STERILE ENVIRONMENT AND MYSTERIOUS INSTRUMENTS...

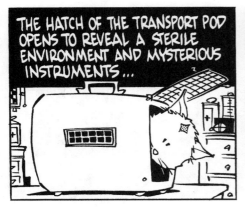

ONE OF THE OTHER LIFE FORMS, THE LEADER, CONDUCTS A BIZARRE EXAMINATION...

THE OTHER, WHOM PEEKABOO RECOGNIZES, STANDS IDLY... USELESS AS ALWAYS EXCEPT AT MEALTIMES

AFTER THE MYSTERIOUS EXAMINATION, THE OTHER LIFE FORMS RETURN PEEKABOO TO THE TRANSPORT POD.

AFTER DOCKING WITH A SHUTTLE CRAFT...

SHE IS RELEASED INTO THE WORLD SHE KNOWS, SHAKEN BUT UNHARMED.

AN ABDUCTEE SUPPORT GROUP SOFTENS THE ROUGH EDGES.

47

ROSE IS ROSE

KITE'S EYE VIEW

ROSE'S INTERPRETATION OF WHAT HAPPENS AS SHE ENTERS A CAMERA'S VIEWFINDER

SMILE, ROSE...

CLICK

I'M GOING TO LOOK UGLY ANYWAY! AT LEAST THIS WAY I FEEL IN CONTROL!

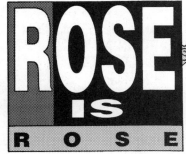

THE EVOLUTION OF GARLIC BREATH

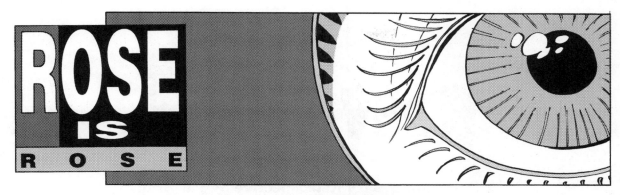

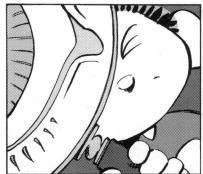

Rosy Oldies

A 15th Anniversary Retrospective by Pat Brady

My first attempts at cartooning happened in church. I was five years old and my parents allowed me to bring drawing materials to church on Sunday. I would sit on the kneeling rail and, facing the back of the church, place my drawing paper on the church pew. It wasn't perfect, but it was a pretty good first drawing table. I happily drew cartoons during the entire Catholic Mass. The people in the pew facing me had a good view of my work, and their smiles served as excellent feedback. On several occasions the priest saw me and laughed. He nicknamed me "Pasquale." So far he hasn't demanded any royalties.

In the first *Rose is Rose* samples I sent to syndicates, the characters looked radically different from the way they look now. They were just heads, hands, and feet. No bodies. It's the way I used to draw people back in my church-pew drawing days. All the syndicates that saw these samples rejected them except for United Feature Syndicate. UFS liked the theme but not the art. They asked me if I would be willing to redo the samples, but with more human-looking characters. Of course I said yes. Thank goodness!

Here are Jimbo and Rose in one of the first samples.

In 1982, prior to *Rose is Rose*, I developed a comic strip I called *Dreamer*. It was rejected by every syndicate that saw it, but in many ways its heart goes on in *Rose is Rose*.

Dreamer

Dreamer © 1982 Pat Brady

Rose is Rose

© 1995 United Feature Syndicate, Inc.

On April 16, 1984, this first *Rose is Rose* strip appeared in about thirty daily newspapers.

For the first seven years of syndication Pasquale spoke in a phonetic language I dubbed "Pasqualian." This strip from May 15, 1984, is typical.

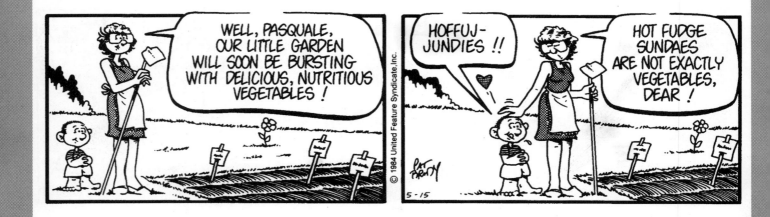

I loved using the phonetic language, but I recognized the risk of it becoming tedious if I let Pasquale continue with it forever. So on August 9, 1991, I reluctantly allowed Pasquale to begin speaking English clearly. Some readers were happy about it, others were disappointed. For me, the change made way for lots of new ideas and new directions for the strip to take.

Pasquale's selfish cousin, Clem, provides what I like to think is a good counterbalance to Pasquale's sweetness. Some readers love Clem, others write to me with demands that he be punished or in some way get his comeuppance. I enjoy drawing Clem more than any other character. Clem's first offense was on July 27, 1987.

I didn't want to lose touch with the phonetic language entirely, so I allowed Mimi, Pasquale's next-door neighbor who spoke only in "peeps," to one day suddenly pick up where Pasquale had left off. Here are three strips showing Mimi on the day of her birth, December 11, 1985, and the evolution of her speech over a span of about six years. . . .

After Pasquale outgrew his phonetic language, Mimi grew into it on September 10, 1991.

Pasquale's Guardian Angel opened up new possibilities all around. Unbound by earthly laws of physics, his character gives me vast fields to play in. Pasquale became aware of him on January 15, 1990.

I love cats and have lived with many, but after developing a bad allergy I now am able to live with only the cartoon kind. I like to think of Peekaboo's diamond forehead as a sign of enlightenment and peace. Peekaboo adopted the Gumbo family in this strip on May 9, 1992.

Of all the themes I've explored in *Rose is Rose*, the one that generates the most fervent and positive response from both male and female readers is the emergence of Rose's alter ego, Vicki the Biker. Vicki seems to touch everybody's wild side in a good way. Here's how she looked when she first emerged on August 29, 1994 (above), and the way she looked the most recent time I drew her. She keeps changing and looks a little different every time. Hey, you got a problem with that?

A lot of *Rose is Rose* readers want to know whether I'm a man or a woman. I'm a man. I'm not embarrassed by the question unless I'm asked in person.

—Pat Brady

Pat Brady was born in 1947 in Louisville, Kentucky, and grew up in Kentucky, Georgia, Florida, Indiana, Kansas, and Illinois. After earning a bachelor's degree from the University of Wisconsin at Whitewater, where he majored in art, Pat held a variety of jobs including social worker, draftsman, commercial artist, and illustrator.

Pat has drawn cartoons since the age of five. He started submitting his cartoons to editors at the age of eleven.

Rose is Rose has been nominated four times for the Reuben Award for Best Newspaper Comic Strip by the National Cartoonists Society. Pat was nominated for the Reuben Award for Outstanding Cartoonist of the Year by the National Cartoonists Society in 1998.

Pat lives in the Midwest.

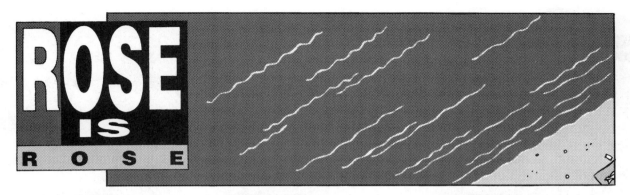

CLEM FEELS THE SWIFT JUSTICE OF A GARLIC BREATH BALLOON.

CLICK
CLICK
CLICK
CLICK

SOPHISTICATED VIEWERS PREFER
THE RAIN CHANNEL

THE LEAF CHANNEL HAS SOME COLORFUL VARIETY SHOWS NOW AND THEN.

I HAVEN'T SEEN THE SNOW CHANNEL FOR A WHILE.

THE NIGHT CHANNEL ALWAYS RUNS MYSTERIES.

CREAK

BUMP

WHOEVER IS HOLDING THE REMOTE CONTROL IS REALLY SLOW.

MIMI, IT WOULD BE MORE POLITE TO SAY, "PLEASE PASS THE NOSE!"

GRAB

71

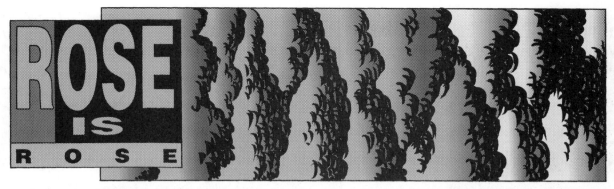

IN THE WILD KINGDOM, THE BRUSSELS SPROUT OFTEN ESCAPES EVEN THE HUNGRIEST PREDATOR

PEEKABOO'S FLIGHT TO THE LAP OF ANOTHER LIFE-FORM REQUIRES EXTENSIVE PRELAUNCH FIDGETING.

FIDGET FIDGET FIDGET

AS THE LAUNCH COUNTDOWN REACHES ITS FINAL SECONDS...

FIDGET FIDGET FIDGET FIDGET FIDGET FIDGET FIDGET FIDGET FIDGET FIDGET FIDGET FIDGET FIDGET

A LAST-MINUTE DELAY TO CLEAN THE LAUNCH VEHICLE IS NOT UNCOMMON.

PEEKABOO'S PRELAUNCH FIDGETING RESUMES, IN PREPARATION FOR HER FLIGHT TO ROSE'S LAP.

FIDGET FIDGET FIDGET

HER ENGINES MUST REACH "CRITICAL FIDGET MASS" BEFORE...

FIDGET FIDGET FIDGET FIDGET FIDGET FIDGET FIDGET FID

THE LAUNCH WINDOW CLOSES.

WE'VE GOT A PROBLEM!

GOOD JOB! HERE'S A DOLLAR!

I SUPPOSE YOU WANT HALF.

HOW CRUDE. I HELPED BECAUSE YOU WERE GETTING A BLISTER.

IF YOU SHUT YOUR EYES IN FRONT OF A MIRROR...

YOU CAN'T PROVE YOUR REFLECTION IS THERE.

THERE ARE A LOT OF THINGS YOU CAN'T PROVE.

HOW DO I KNOW HE'S NOT THE REAL PASQUALE AND I'M NOT THE REFLECTION?

WHAT IF IT TURNS OUT THAT THEY ARE THE REAL PEOPLE AND WE ARE THE REFLECTIONS?

STOP IT! YOU'RE FREAKING ME OUT!

WHY DID I HAVE TO GET A HAIRCUT RIGHT BEFORE **SCHOOL PICTURE DAY?**

HAIRCUTS ALWAYS MAKES MY **NOSE** AND **EARS** LOOK **BIG!**

SCHOOL BUS

I HOPE I'M NOT THE **ONLY** KID WITH A HAIRCUT TODAY!

SCHOOL

OOL BUS

:WHEW:

SQUEAK SQUEAK

HIGHLIGHT MARKER PLEASURE SYNDROME

HERE'S YOUR RECEIPT FOR THE HIGHLIGHT MARKERS!

I'LL DO THE PRICE YELLOW, THE SALES TAX BLUE, THE TOTAL PINK AND THE THANK YOU GREEN!

SQUEAK SQUEAK

HIGHLIGHT MARKER MANIA

WHY NEWSPAPERS ARE BETTER THAN TV NEWS: REASON #1...

WHY NEWSPAPERS ARE BETTER THAN TV NEWS: REASONS #2 AND 3...

WHY NEWSPAPERS ARE BETTER THAN TV NEWS: REASON #4...

WHY NEWSPAPERS ARE BETTER THAN TV NEWS: REASON #5...

THEY'RE AUTOMATICALLY **RECORDED** FOR VIEWING AT YOUR CONVENIENCE

WHY NEWSPAPERS ARE BETTER THAN TV NEWS: REASON #6...

WHY, THANK YOU!

YOU NEVER GET A BEAR HUG FOR TURNING ON THE TV

WHY NEWSPAPERS ARE BETTER THAN TV NEWS: REASON #7...

EVERYONE CAN CHOOSE DIFFERENT CHANNELS AND STILL STAY IN THE SAME ROOM TOGETHER

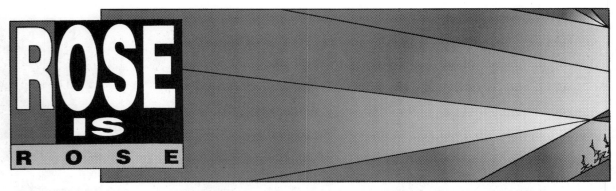

ROSE IS ROSE

THIS IS SCOUT SHIP #1 REPORTING VISUAL CONTACT WITH POSSIBLE LANDING SITE. OVER.

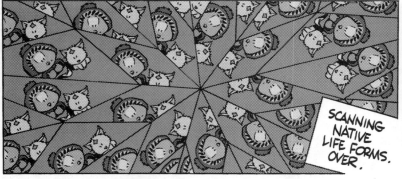

SCANNING NATIVE LIFE FORMS. OVER.

MAYDAY!! RETREAT!! RE—

ANY SIGN OF SNOWFLAKES, PASQUALE?

PEEKABOO ATE THE FIRST ONE! THE REST ARE FLOATING BACK UP!

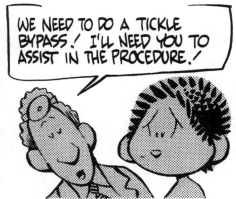

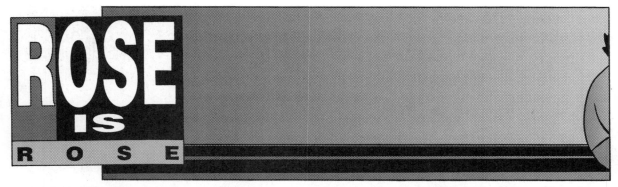

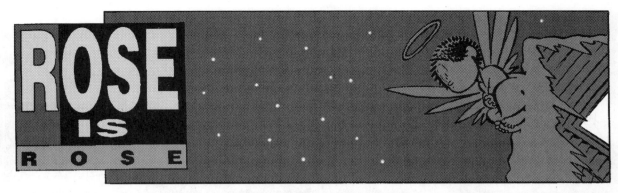

YOO KANT LETGO OF A NOZE FOR A MINNIT!

MOBILE'S EYE VIEW

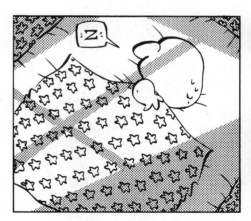

SLEEPSNEEZERS WAKE UP KNOWING SOMETHING HAPPENED, BUT THEY'RE NOT SURE WHAT

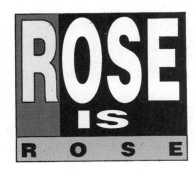

95

WHERE ARE YOU GOING? OUT!

I'D APPRECIATE A MOMENT TO GET MY WORRIES ORGANIZED!

WHERE ARE YOU GOING, AND TO DO WHAT WITH WHOM?

I'M GOING TO THE BACKYARD TO BUILD A SNOWMAN WITH COUSIN CLEM!

FINE...

JUST MAKE SURE YOU STAY WITHIN A THREE-WORRY RADIUS OF ME!

I'VE ALWAYS LOVED WATCHING THE ELECTRIC METER DIAL SPIN!

THE STEADY SPINNING EXUDES A PEACEFUL STABILITY, GIVING RISE TO A QUIET CONFIDENCE IN THE ORDER OF THE UNIVERSE!

WE PAY WAY TOO LITTLE FOR ELECTRICITY!

ROSE, YOU'VE BEEN GAZING INTO THE METER AGAIN!

BILLS

I WAS PLAYING WITH MY CAT AND SHE ACCIDENTALLY SCRATCHED ME, DOCTOR!

IT'S NOT TOO BAD, MRS. GUMBO, BUT IT MIGHT LEAVE A TINY SCAR!

SCAR? ♡

ROSE, WHAT DID THE DOCTOR SAY ABOUT THE SCRATCH PEEKABOO GAVE YOU?

KNOCK KNOCK

HE SAID IT MIGHT LEAVE A SCAR!

DOCTORS DON'T KNOW EVERYTHING!

COMMENTS LIKE THAT CAN INTERFERE WITH A PATIENT'S PROGRESS!

I KNOW YOU DIDN'T MEAN TO SCRATCH ME, PEEKABOO!

JUST BE CAREFUL WITH THOSE CLAWS...

AND RESPECT THEM AS YOUR OWN BLESSINGS OF INDEPENDENCE AND FREEDOM!

CLICK CLICK CLICK

98

PRETTY WOMAN CROSSING

THERE'S JUST SOMETHING ABOUT WEARING A NEW HAT!

I REGRET THAT MY EFFORTS HAVE NOT MET YOUR CRITERIA FOR DINING EXCELLENCE.

IN THE FUTURE I HOPE TO DEVELOP MENUS THAT MORE RESPECTFULLY REFLECT YOUR PREFERENCES.

I KNOW SHE'S REALLY MAD WHEN SHE TALKS THAT NICE!

MUNCH MUNCH MUNCH MUNCH MUNCH

MOMMA?! MAY I HAVE A DRINK OF WATER PLEASE?

SHUFFLE SHUFFLE SHUFFLE

Z

HE DIDN'T WANT THE WATER?

SOMETIMES HE JUST NEEDS THE SHUFFLE!

ROSE IS ROSE

BLESSINGS AND BENEFITS OF A SMALL KITCHEN: CHAPTER #1

YOU'RE IN EACH OTHER'S WAY SO MUCH IT FEELS LIKE DANCING.

PARDON ME.

EXCUSEZ-MOI.

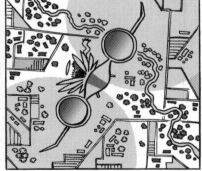

A WORLD CLASS NAPPER NOT ONLY CAN SNOOZE ATOP A REFRIGERATOR, BUT CAN DISPLAY PERFECT FORM WHEN FALLING OFF, SOUND ASLEEP

TOUCH-TESTING A LAP CAN AVOID A LOT OF PROBLEMS.

MAY I EAT IN THE TV ROOM? MY FAVORITE SHOW'S ON.!

DINNERTIME IS FAMILY CONVERSATION TIME!

MAY I VIDEOTAPE IT FOR LATER?

SURE!

WHIRRR COME BACK HERE!

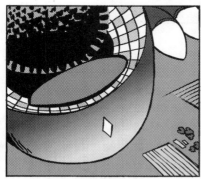

THIS IS MY "LET THINGS BE" TREE.

SOMEHOW, WHEN I LEAN AGAINST IT, I'M ABLE TO JUST LET THINGS BE.

MY FIRST CHOICE WOULD HAVE BEEN A "FIX EVERYTHING" TREE.

WHEN I'M ANXIOUS ABOUT THINGS, I LEAN AGAINST MY "LET THINGS BE" TREE.

AFTER A WHILE, I'M ABLE TO JUST LET THOSE THINGS BE.

SOME THINGS NEED AN EXTRA LEAN.

I FEEL SO MUCH BETTER AFTER LEANING AGAINST MY "LET THINGS BE" TREE.

I WONDER WHETHER ANYONE ELSE HAS A "LET THINGS BE" TREE!

SHE'S ANNOYING, BUT I'LL JUST LET HER BE.

ROSE IS ROSE

SNOWFLAKES ARE LIKE TINY PIECES OF PURE QUIET.

THEY REALLY SHOULD BE CALLED QUIETFLAKES.

WE'D SAY, "THE WEATHER FORECAST CALLS FOR THREE INCHES OF QUIET TODAY."

WE'D WEAR QUIETSUITS...

...BUILD QUIETMEN...

...THROW QUIETBALLS...

OBVIOUSLY WE WOULDN'T HEAR THEM COMING.

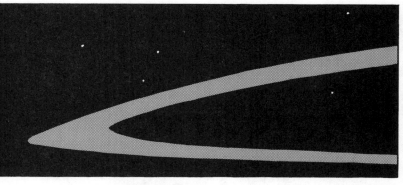

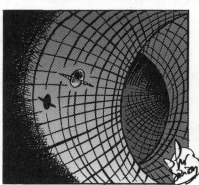

A DEMONSTRATION OF MIMI, THE MOM MAGNET

WE HEAR WITH OUR EARS MIMI, NOT OUR NOSES!

POYN CHERNO ZATMEE!

HEER BEDDER?

I ADMIT IT... I CAN HEAR YOU BETTER WHEN I POINT MY NOSE AT YOU!

I TOL-JA!

THIS PARTITIONED DINNER PLATE WILL KEEP YOUR PEAS FROM TOUCHING YOUR POTATOES, AS YOU INSIST!

OF COURSE, EVERYTHING WILL GET MIXED TOGETHER INSIDE YOUR BELLY!

I'LL BRING UP YOUR "PARTITIONED BELLY" IDEA AT THE NEXT ANGEL CONFERENCE, BUT I'M NOT PROMISING ANYTHING!

BEEP!

BEEP!

BEEP! BEEP!

A-OOO-GA!!

AN A-OOO-GA NOSE: REASON TO ADMIRE A DADDY # 723

LET'S SEE... I'LL STOP AT THE CLEANERS ON MY WAY TO...

WHOA!

THAT FIRST SPRING BREEZE ALWAYS CATCHES ME BY SURPRISE.

AFTER ROAMING THE EARTH, WE, THE DESCENDANTS OF DINOSAURS, HAVE RETURNED TO OUR PRIMORDIAL HOME!

SMELLS MUSTY, TOO!

SHALL WE LET OUT A TERRIFYING ROAR?

THAT'S OUR DINOSAUR NATURE, ISN'T IT?

IT FEELS LIKE A HUNDRED MILLION YEARS SINCE I HEARD THAT SOUND!

SPRING

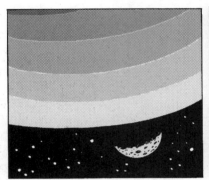

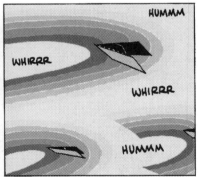

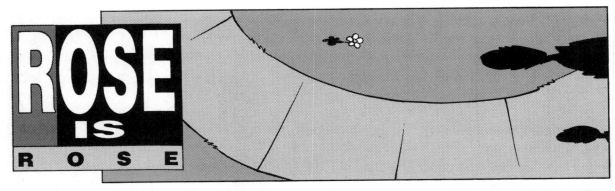

WHEN YOUR HAT FLIES OFF, THAT MEANS YOU'RE SURPRISED!

IT DOES?!

OH, ABSOLUTELY! THE PHENOMENON IS WELL DOCUMENTED IN COMICS!

WOW! I'M SURPRISED! I THOUGHT THE WIND BLEW IT OFF!

SEE? I TOLD YOU YOU WERE SURPRISED!

I AGREE WITH MOMMA!

ABOUT WHAT?

SHE SAYS YOU'RE THE SMARTEST MAN SHE EVER MET!

UH-OH! WHAT'S HAPPENING TO MY FACE?

I SEEM TO HAVE STUMBLED INTO SOME SORT OF...

...FROWN FIELD...

YOU'RE TRYING TO MAKE ME SMILE BY PRETENDING THERE'S A "FROWN FIELD" AROUND ME!

WELL, I'M NOT FALLING FOR IT! THERE'S NO SUCH THING!

SMOOCHER FENDER BENDER

115

THE FIRST WATER BALLOON OF SPRING APPEARS IN THE VERY SPOT WHERE THE LAST ONE WAS SEEN IN ONE AUTUMN.

GOOD NIGHT, MOMMA...

TOMORROW IS THE LAST DAY OF SCHOOL, REMEMBER?

I *DO* REMEMBER!

BUS STOP

IT'S THE LAST DAY OF SCHOOL... THE LAST DAY OF SCHOOL...

TAPPITY TAPPITY

WAIT! THAT'S NOT THE SCHOOL BUS! I'M ONLY *DREAMING*?! OH, NO!!

WAKE UP, SLEEPYHEAD! TODAY IS THE LAST DAY OF SCHOOL!

OH, YES!!

I'M RUSHED THIS MORNING, PASQUALE! I HAVE ONLY A FEW MINUTES TO FIX BREAKFAST...

ARE SCRAMBLED EGGS OKAY?

LET'S HAVE APPLES AND MINUTES!

I GUESS THERE'S MORE THAN ONE KIND OF HEALTHY BREAKFAST!

I LIKE MY MINUTES SUNNYSIDE UP!

SEE? YOU DID FIT!

RAIN GEAR

BUS

119

THERE'S ALWAYS ROOM FOR TWO
IN A HAMMOCK

WHY BOTHER, ROSE? YOU FALL ASLEEP IN THE FIRST TEN MINUTES OF EVERY MOVIE YOU EVER RENT!

THIS ONE LOOKS GOOD!

WE CAN SAVE AN EXTRA TRIP IF YOU PUT IT IN THE DROP BOX ON YOUR WAY OUT OF THE STORE.

PAT PAT PAT

LET'S SEE... WHAT BOOK WOULD YOU LIKE ME TO READ TONIGHT?

INVISIBLE BOOKS ARE MY FAVORITE KIND!

ONCE UPON A TIME...

"ANY LAP IN A STORM."

I NEVER ASK PASQUALE, "WOULD YOU LIKE A VEGETABLE?" HE'D SAY NO!

I CLEVERLY LIMIT HIS CHOICES BY ASKING, "WOULD YOU PREFER SPINACH OR PEAS?"

HE HAS TO CHOOSE ONE OR THE OTHER! SEE?

MOMMA, WOULD YOU PREFER THAT I DRIVE THE CAR OR PLAY ON THE ROOF?

MY PROBLEM IS, I HAVE ONLY ENOUGH MODELING CLAY TO MAKE ONE THING AT A TIME...

FOR EXAMPLE, FIRST I'LL MAKE A CATERPILLAR...

THEN I'LL CHANGE IT TO...

A BUTTERFLY!

I RUN INTO THE SAME PROBLEM!